T0015733

Introduction

Regarded as the world's healthiest cuisine, Asian food is traditionally cooked quickly to conserve fuel and energy. Preparation can be meticulously time-consuming but also contains the essence of simplicity. Once most ingredients are peeled, chopped, sliced, minced, shaped and shredded with concentration and rhythmic ease with a Chinese cleaver on a wooden board, the wok, a bamboo steamer and long chopsticks or a wooden spoon will take care of the rest.

All varieties of rice are good for you. With the benefits of wholegrains, brown rice is the most nutritious rice variety but it takes longer to cook unless you use a quick cooking variety.

There are a few different ways of cooking rice, depending on what you're making and how much time you have. It's supposed to be easy but many will admit they can never get perfect fluffy rice. A rice cooker takes a lot of the guess work out of this task and there are many reasonably priced models available.

Probably the simplest method is boiling, but there are a few tricks to getting this right. One cup of raw rice makes about two cups when cooked. To boil, bring about eight cups of water to boiling point, then add the rice. Make sure you then turn the heat down to a gentle boil and let it cook uncovered for about 15 minutes for white rice and about 30 minutes for brown rice.

The marinating of meat, fish, poultry and meat is common. Where ingredients have different textures, but must be cooked simultaneously in a wok, blanching, steaming and poaching are often carried out before stir-frying.

Dried food, for example shrimps and fungus, are soaked in water, with the soaking liquid then used as stock. The hanging and air-drying of poultry following marinating and, sometimes, steaming, ensures that the skin becomes crispy after roasting or deep-frying, just as with Peking duck.

Asian cuisine is local, authentic, and traditional. It is rich in taste from the herbs and spices used in the preparations. Asian cuisine features multicultural dishes from diverse cultures and origins from Southeast Asia, Europe, America, and around the globe.

Asian food contains a lot of vegetables and contains a large variety of spices that contributes a lot of taste to its dishes. Authentic Asian food has the best combination of salty, sweet, and spicy with food that has a variety of textures, which makes it interesting to the taste buds.

Starters

Spring Rolls

Makes 32 rolls

500 g/1 lb 2 oz minced chicken
¼ of a Chinese cabbage, finely chopped
½ red capsicum/red bell pepper seeded and thinly sliced
4 mushrooms, thinly sliced
1 tablespoon soy sauce
1 tablespoon oyster sauce
2 teaspoons cornflour
1 tablespoon water
2 tablespoons oil
2 teaspoons fresh ginger, finely chopped
1 small onion, finely chopped
1 packet frozen spring roll wrappers
Oil for deep frying

🍜 Prepare all vegetables, combine the 2 sauces and mix cornflour and water together.

🍜 Heat wok and add 2 tablespoons of oil.

🍜 Add ginger and onion and cook until onion is pale gold in color.

🍜 Add minced chicken and cook until white all over (about 2 minutes), toss in vegetables and stir-fry for one minute, mixing chicken through vegetables.

🍜 Pour in combined sauces, tossing to mix through.

🍜 Push mixture to one side and add blended cornflour to juices in the base of wok. As juices thicken, stir and toss through vegetables.

🍜 Spread mixture out onto a flat tray to cool.

🍜 Wrap one heaped tablespoon chicken mixture in each wrapper according to packet directions.

🍜 Wipe out wok, heat and add fresh oil to approximately 5 cm/2 in deep.

🍜 Heat oil and fry rolls a few at a time until gold color and crisp.

🍜 Drain on paper towels.

🍜 Serve hot.

Sesame Prawn/Shrimp Triangles with Chilli Dipping Sauce

Serves 4

125 g/4 oz cooked peeled prawns/shrimps - defrost if frozen
1 clove garlic, chopped
2 tablespoons beaten egg
1 teaspoon cornflour
½ teaspoon sesame oil
A few drops of light soy sauce
3 slices of white bread
2 tablespoons sesame seeds
Peanut oil for deep-frying

Dipping Sauce

1 teaspoon fresh root ginger, finely chopped
2 tablespoons hot chilli sauce
Juice of ½ lime

🦐 Blend prawns/shrimps, garlic, egg, cornflour, oil and soy sauce to a paste in a food processor. Alternatively, grind prawns/shrimps with a pestle and mortar, then mix with the other ingredients.

🦐 Spread one side of each slice of bread evenly with prawn paste, sprinkle with sesame seeds, remove crusts and cut into 4 triangles.

🦐 To make dipping sauce, mix together ginger, chilli sauce and lime juice, then set aside.

🦐 Heat 2 tablespoons of peanut oil in a large frying-pan over a medium to high heat.

🦐 Add half the prawn triangles, prawn-side down and fry for 4–5 minutes on each side, until deep golden.

🦐 Drain on kitchen towels and keep warm while you cook the remaining prawn triangles.

🦐 Serve with dipping sauce.

Chinese Dumplings

Makes 40

125 g /4 oz minced pork
vegetable oil
250 g/9 oz prawn meat, finely chopped
4 water chestnuts, chopped
2 spring onions/scallions, chopped
½ teaspoon salt
2 teaspoons soy sauce
40 egg wonton wrappers

🥘 Sauté pork in 2 teaspoons of oil in a pan for about 1 minute.

🥘 Add remaining ingredients with the exception of the wonton wrappers and the rest of the oil. Stir, combining completely.

🥘 Remove from heat and allow to cool to room temperature.

☕ To make dumplings, place a teaspoon of the mixture into the centre of each wonton wrapper. Brush edges with a little water, pull corners to the centre and pinch edges together to seal mixture inside.

☕ Heat enough oil in pan or wok for deep- frying. Drop in wontons 8–10 at a time, and fry until golden (about 2–3 minutes).

☕ Drain on kitchen paper.

☕ Dumplings can be kept warm in a slow oven for about 1 hour.

☕ Serve with soy, sweet chilli, plum or chilli plum sauce.

Peking Spring Onion/ Scallion Pancakes

Serves 4

2 eggs
6 spring onions/scallions, sliced finely
170 g/6 oz plain flour
2 rashers bacon, finely chopped
1 cup/8 oz chicken stock
pinch of salt
3 tablespoons vegetable oil

⚭ Beat eggs well, then add spring onions/scallions, plain flour, bacon, stock and salt and combine to form a smooth batter.

⚭ Put a 25 cm/10 in frying-pan on medium heat, add 2 teaspoons of oil to spread over base of pan.

⚭ Pour a quarter of the batter into the pan ensuring it covers the base.

⚭ When pancake edge is golden, turn pancake carefully until cooked.

⚭ Remove and repeat the procedure 3 more times with extra oil to make 4 pancakes.

⚭ Serve hot.

Chicken Satay (Sate Ayam)

Makes about 12

12 bamboo skewers
500 g/1 lb 2 oz chicken thigh fillets, diced (beef, lamb
and pork can also be used)
2 tablespoons peanut oil
2 tablespoons sweet soy sauce (Kecap Manis)
1 tablespoon soy sauce
1 garlic clove, crushed
Peanut sauce, to serve

🍲 Soak the bamboo skewers in cold water for 15–20
minutes.

🍲 Thread diced chicken onto the bamboo skewers
and arrange in a large, shallow dish.

🍲 Combine the peanut oil, soy sauces and garlic in a
bowl and stir to combine.

🍲 Pour the marinade over the chicken and leave to
marinate in the refrigerator for 1–2 hours.

🍲 Cook the satays on a barbecue for 10–15 minutes,
or until cooked through.

🍲 Serve with peanut sauce.

Quick Peanut Sauce (Saus Kacang Cepat)

60 g/2 oz crunchy peanut butter
60 ml/2 fl oz water
2 teaspoons sambal oelek
1 teaspoon kecap manis (sweet soy sauce)
2 teaspoons lemon juice

🥥 Combine the peanut butter and water in a small saucepan.

🥥 Stir over low heat until the sauce thickens.

🥥 Remove from the heat and stir in the sambal oelek and kecap manis and allow to cool before adding lemon juice.

Chicken and Sweet Corn Soup

Serves 6

500 g/1 lb 2 oz of minced chicken
Large pinch of salt
2 egg whites, beaten to froth
6 cups chicken stock
400 g/14 oz creamed corn
2 tablespoons cornflour blended with 3 ½ tablespoons water
2 tablespoons dry sherry
1 dessertspoon light soy sauce
1 teaspoon sesame oil

Garnish

Thin slices of Chinese smoked ham or cooked bacon

🍲 Cook minced chicken in a pan on medium heat till white.

🍲 Stir in cooked minced chicken, sherry, soy sauce and sesame oil and simmer, stirring, for 3 minutes.

☕ Bring stock to the boil, add corn and return soup to the boil.

☕ Thicken with cornflour mix, stirring for about 1 minute.

☕ Stir in cooked minced chicken, sherry, soy sauce and sesame oil and simmer, stirring, for 3 minutes.

☕ Use a fork to whisk the egg whites in a small bowl. Gradually pour the egg whites into the soup, stirring constantly, Cook for 2 minutes or until white ribbons swirl though the soup.

☕ Serve soup garnished with finely chopped Chinese smoked ham or cooked bacon bits. If you can't buy Chinese ham, substitute with any ham.

Miso Soup

Serves 2

There are many varieties of miso available in Japan, but outside Japan the most frequently found varieties are red miso, brown miso and white miso.

Brown miso has a well-balanced flavor and aroma; red miso has a stronger flavor; white miso is sweeter and less salty.

4 cups super dashi
2 tablespoons light brown miso paste mixed well with
1 tablespoon mirin
¼ small packet silken tofu, cubed
1 pinch of dried wakame-seaweed soaked in water
1 spring onion/scallion stem, chopped

🥣 Bring super dashi to boil in a saucepan.

🥣 Add miso and dissolve over low heat.

🥣 Add tofu and wakame and simmer for a couple of minutes.

🥣 Pour the soup into individual bowls.

🥣 Sprinkle spring onion/scallion over the top.

Meat

Chinese Five Spice Pork Belly

Serves 6

2 tablespoons sunflower or peanut oil
2 small cloves garlic, crushed
2 tablespoons Chinese five spice powder
3 tablespoons soy sauce
6 tablespoons dry or medium sherry
2 spring onions/scallions, finely chopped
Pared orange rind, cut into strips
Juice of 2 large oranges
Salt and black pepper
750 g/26 oz pork belly
15 g/½ oz butter, chilled and cubed

To Garnish

Fresh snipped chives

☕ In a small bowl, mix together oil, garlic, five spice powder, soy sauce, sherry and spring onions/scallions to make a marinade. Add half the orange rind and juice and season with salt and black pepper.

☕ Put pork into a non-metallic bowl, pour the marinade over and cover, or place meat and marinade in a roasting bag, tie bag well and shake. Refrigerate for at least 2 hours, or up to 24 hours, turning the meat or shaking the bag once or twice.

☕ Preheat the oven to 190°C/375°F. Transfer pork and marinade to a roasting tin, loosely cover with foil and cook for 30 minutes. Take off the foil, turn fillet and cook for a further 15 minutes. Cover and leave to stand for 10 minutes. Alternatively, roast in the bag for 45 minutes, then leave to stand for 10 minutes, still in the bag, with the oven door ajar and the heat turned off.

☕ Slice the meat. Pour the cooking juices into a small saucepan, add rest of orange juice and heat gently. Whisk in butter and adjust the seasoning. Serve the slices of meat with the sauce poured over.

☕ Garnish with chives

Pork and Hokkien Noodle Stir-Fry

Serves 4

500 g/1 lb 2 oz pork stir-fry strips
100 g/3 ½ oz bamboo shoots, sliced
400 g/14 oz stir-fry vegetables, sliced - for example cabbage, carrots, celery and capsicum/bell pepper
2 tablespoons peanut oil
2 cloves garlic, crushed
1 onion, sliced
500 g/1 lb 2 oz hokkien or egg noodles
1 cup chicken stock or salt-reduced stir-fry sauce
2 teaspoons cornflour
1 tablespoon Shaoxing rice wine or dry sherry (optional)
2 tablespoons reduced-salt soy sauce

🍲 Gather equipment, sauces and fresh ingredients before starting to cook. Slice pork and vegetables into even, thin strips or cut into even bite-size pieces.

🍲 Heat wok or non-stick frying-pan until hot. Drizzle in oil and swirl to lightly glaze and coat the bottom and sides. Stir-fry garlic and onion for about 15 seconds until fragrant.

☕ Stir-fry pork in 1–2 batches until just cooked. Allow pan to reheat between batches. Remove pork from pan.

☕ Add a little more oil to the wok. Stir-fry harder vegetables in hot oil for about 30 seconds to 1 minute or until bright and hot, but still crisp. Noodles (or rice) can be added at this stage if desired. Save any softer, leafy and easy-to-wilt vegetables such as bean sprouts and herbs until the end. Return pork to the hot wok and lightly combine with vegetables.

☕ Make a well by pushing pork and vegetables to the side. Add stir-fry sauce, or chicken stock combined with cornflour, and pour into pan. Stir until it simmers, toss meat and vegetables through the sauce, and heat.

☕ Combine any remaining ingredients including softer, leafy vegetables and herbs.

☕ Taste and adjust the flavor as required with rice wine or sherry and soy sauce. Garnish and serve immediately.

Red Roasted Pork

Serves 4

500 g/1 lb 2 oz pork fillet
1 tablespoon sugar
1 tablespoon light soy sauce
1 ½ teaspoons black bean sauce
2 teaspoons salt
2 ½ tablespoons dry sherry
2 cloves garlic, crushed
1 teaspoon five spice powder
1 teaspoon red food coloring
1 tablespoon honey
1 tablespoon sesame oil

🍲 Cut pork into long strips, 4 cm/1.5 in thick.

🍲 In a bowl combine sugar, soy sauce, black bean sauce, salt, sherry, garlic, five spice powder and food coloring. Add pork strips to marinate for at least 3 hours but preferably overnight, turning occasionally.

🍲 Preheat oven to 200°C/400°F. Transfer pork from marinade into a roasting pan and roast in oven for 15 minutes in a little oil.

🍲 Mix sesame oil with honey and spoon it over pork to roast for a further 15 minutes. After pork is cool, cut into thin slivers. Serve hot or cold.

Sizzling Beef

Serves 4

500 g/1 lb 2 oz rump steak, trimmed of any excess fat and cut into thin strips
2 tablespoons soy sauce
2 tablespoons rice wine or sherry
1 ½ tablespoons cornflour
1 teaspoon sugar
3 tablespoons peanut oil
150 g/5 oz broccoli, cut into bite-size pieces
1 large red capsicum/bell pepper, deseeded and cut into thin strips
2 cloves garlic, crushed
3 tablespoons oyster sauce
200 g/7 oz fresh bean sprouts
Salt and black pepper

🍲 Put steak, soy sauce, rice wine or sherry, cornflour and sugar into a non-metallic bowl and mix thoroughly.

🍲 Heat 1 tablespoon of oil in a wok or large heavy-based frying-pan, add one third of the beef mixture and stir-fry over a high heat for 2–3 minutes until browned. Remove and cook remaining beef in 2 more batches, adding a little more oil if necessary.

🍲 Heat remaining oil in wok, then add broccoli and 6 tablespoons of water. Stir-fry for 5 minutes, then add capsicum/bell pepper and garlic and stir-fry for a further 2–3 minutes, until the broccoli is tender but still firm to the bite.

🍲 Stir in oyster sauce, return the beef to the wok and add bean sprouts. Toss over a high heat for 2 minutes or until beef is piping hot and bean sprouts have softened slightly.

🍲 Add salt and pepper to taste.

Sweet and Sour Pork

Serves 4-6

400 g/14 oz lean pork, cubed
Pinch of salt
½ teaspoon ground black pepper
2 tablespoons dry sherry
1 egg, lightly beaten
4 tablespoons cornflour
Vegetable oil for frying

Sauce

1 small green/red capsicum/bell pepper
1 fresh red chilli, seeded and finely chopped
2 cloves garlic, crushed
1 teaspoon fresh ginger, grated
3 tablespoons tomato sauce or 1 tablespoon tomato paste
1 tablespoon soy sauce
3 tablespoons honey
1 tablespoon cornflour
1 small can pineapple pieces, drained and juice reserved
Vegetable oil for frying

🥥 Prepare vegetables for sauce. Cut capsicum / bell pepper and onion into a large dice. Put pork cubes in a bowl, sprinkle with salt and pepper, add sherry, mix and marinate for 30 minutes.

🥥 Toss pork cubes in a bag containing cornflour then dip pork in beaten egg and toss in cornflour again. Heat some oil in a preheated wok or heavy-based pan and deep-fry pork until brown. Drain on paper towels and reserve.

🥥 Drain off all oil except for about 2 tablespoons, heat and add onions, capsicum / bell pepper, chilli, garlic and ginger and stir-fry for 2 minutes. Mix tomato sauce or paste, soy sauce, honey, cornflour and juice from pineapple.

🥥 When smooth, add to wok and stir until thickened. Add water if too thick. Stir in pork and drained pineapple pieces, heat through and serve.

Dry-Fried Beef Curry (Rendang Daging)

Serves 4

¼ cup desiccated (dry unsweetened shredded) coconut
1 ½ tablespoons vegetable oil
1 kg/ 2 lb 3 oz beef, diced
2 cups coconut milk
2 salam leaves
1 stalk lemongrass, white part chopped and the top tied in a knot
Boiled rice, to serve

Paste

3 shallots, chopped
6–8 medium red chillies, deseeded and chopped
2 teaspoons root ginger, chopped
3 garlic cloves, chopped
½ teaspoon galangal powder
1 teaspoon ground turmeric
2 teaspoons peanut oil

🍲 Crush or pound the paste ingredients in a mortar with pestle, or in a food processor. (Add 2 teaspoons peanut oil if using a food processor).

🍲 Dry-fry the desiccated coconut in a saucepan until golden.

🍲 Heat 1 tablespoon oil in a large frying pan. Add half the beef and stir-fry 2–3 minutes, or until the beef is brown. Remove and set aside.

🍲 Add the remaining oil and beef and stir-fry for another 2–3 minutes. Remove and set aside.

🍲 Add the paste and stir-fry for 1 minute.

🍲 Add the coconut milk, salam leaves, lemongrass stalk and beef. Bring to the boil.

🍲 Reduce the heat and simmer uncovered for 1½ hours and or until the liquid has evaporated and beef is tender.

🍲 Serve with boiled rice on the side.

San Choy Bao

Serves 4

1 cup basmati rice
1 small iceberg lettuce
2 tablespoons oil
1 clove garlic, crushed
300 g/10 oz minced pork
100 g/3.5 oz shiitake mushrooms, finely chopped
¼ red capsicum/bell pepper, finely sliced
1 tablespoon mirin
2 teaspoons soy sauce
1 tablespoon oyster sauce
1 teaspoon sugar
3 long spring onions/scallions, chopped
1 cup bean sprouts

☕ Place the rice in a saucepan with 2 cups of water. Bring to the boil, reduce heat to low, cover and cook for 15 minutes. Remove pan from heat, allow to stand, covered, for 10 minutes.

☕ Carefully remove individual leaves from the lettuce, avoiding tearing the leaves. Trim with scissors to make an even rounded cup (not essential).

☕ Heat the oil in a heavy-based frying pan, add the garlic and pork and stir-fry over high heat for 1–2 minutes. Add the mushrooms and capsicum/bell pepper and cook for a further 1–2 minutes.

☕ Add the cooked rice, mirin, soy sauce, oyster sauce and sugar and toss through to combine.

☕ Stir in the spring onions/scallions and bean sprouts, remove from heat and spoon into lettuce cups to serve.

Note: add some chilli if you want a bit of heat.

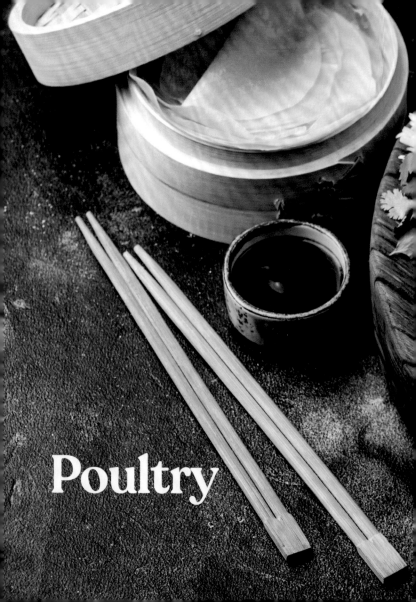

Poultry

Peking Duck

Serves 6

2 kg/4.4 lbs duck
2 tablespoons soy sauce
2 ½ tablespoons brown sugar
1 teaspoon red vinegar

To Serve

Hoisin sauce
1 small cucumber, cut into julienne strips
6 spring onions/scallions

Mandarin Pancakes

4 cups plain flour
Pinch of salt
1 ¼ cups boiling water
Peanut or sesame oil

🥢 Plunge duck into a large pot of boiling water for 3 minutes. Drain it, dry it, truss it and hang it up in an airy room to dry completely overnight.

🥢 Combine soy sauce, brown sugar and vinegar, rub into duck and re-hang for 4 hours. If you can't hang the duck, place on a rack where there is good ventilation. Place drip pan beneath.

🍲 Place duck on a rack on top a roasting pan half filled with hot water and cook in preheated oven at 190°C/375°F for 30 minutes. Lower heat to 150°C/300°F for 1 hour, then adjust to original temperature until skin is crisp and brown all over and the duck is tender.

🍲 Cut spring onions/scallions to the size of the cucumber strips, about 5 cm/2 in.

🍲 To make pancakes, sift flour and salt into a bowl. Make a well in the centre, add boiling water and mix to a stiff dough, kneading until smooth. Cover with a damp cloth and leave to rest 15 minutes.

🍲 On a floured board, shape dough into a roll about 5 cm/2 in in diameter. Cut the roll into 1.5 cm/0.5 in wide slices to roll into pancakes about 8 cm/3.5 in in diameter.

🍲 Sandwich 2 pancakes together with peanut or sesame oil and roll out pancake pairs to 15 cm/6 in. Repeat with remaining dough. Makes 8 pancakes.

🥢 Heat a heavy-based pan on high, but don't let it smoke, before turning it down to a gentle temperature and dry-frying each double pancake for about 1 minute. Pancake should inflate a little and just be slightly marked with brown.

🥢 When cool enough to touch, separate each pancake and fold in half. To keep pancakes hot while carving duck, cover with foil on a warmed dish.

🥢 Carve skin then meat, keeping separate. Arrange on a plate with cucumber. Serve pancakes and spring onion strips or brushes on individual small plates for each diner. Each diner then spreads a little hoisin sauce on the pancakes, tops with some meat then skin, a cucumber matchstick and spring onion to roll up and enjoy.

Duck Salad

Serves 4

2 tablespoons vinegar
2 ½ tablespoons sugar
2 tablespoons peanut oil
2 tablespoons soy sauce
1 teaspoon mustard, home-mixed or prepared
Pinch of salt
125 g/4.4 oz carrot
125 g/4.4 oz cucumber
100 g/3.5 oz bok choy or cabbage
500 g/1 lb 2 oz cooked duck meat

👲 Mix dressing of vinegar, sugar, peanut oil, soy sauce, mustard and salt thoroughly.

👲 Shred carrot and cucumber into paper thin strips with a potato peeler. Cut end off bok choy, wash leaves very carefully and shred as thinly as possible.

👲 Arrange vegetables on a serving plate and top with shredded duck. Add dressing just before serving.

Drunken Chicken

Serves 6

1.5 kg/3.3 lb chicken
2 medium onions
2 teaspoons salt
3 pieces fresh root ginger, peeled and sliced

Water

1 ¼ cups dry sherry
2 teaspoons sugar

🍵 Wash chicken. Quarter onions and place in a pot with salt and ginger. Add chicken with enough hot water to cover and bring to the boil for 5 minutes. Cover and simmer for 15 minutes.

🍵 Transfer chicken to a large non-metallic bowl. Add sherry and sugar to cooking liquid, pour over chicken, rotate several times to ensure chicken is completely immersed and cover tightly with plastic wrap. Refrigerate for 48 hours, stirring and cold basting with marinade occasionally.

🍵 Drain chicken, discarding onions and chop through bone into serving-sized pieces.

🍵 Serve cold.

Balinese-Style Fried Chicken (Ayam Bali)

Serves 4

¼ cup peanut oil
8 small chicken pieces
¾–1 cup coconut milk
2 teaspoons sweet soy sauce (kecap manis)
2 tablespoons lime juice
2 tablespoons lime zest
1 long green chilli, deseeded and sliced
Rice, to serve
Green (French) beans, to serve

Paste

3 shallots/spring onions
2 cloves garlic
2 teaspoons root ginger, chopped
4 medium red chillies, deseeded and chopped
3 candle nuts (or macadamias)
2 teaspoons sweet soy sauce (kecap manis)

🍲 Crush or pound the paste ingredients, except for the kecap manis, in a mortar with pestle or in a food processor. Add the kecap manis and stir to combine.

🍲 Heat the oil in a wok or frying pan. Add the chicken in two batches and cook until golden.

🍲 Remove the chicken and drain on kitchen paper. Pour off and discard the excess oil.

🍲 Cook the paste for 1–2 minutes. Add the coconut milk, kecap manis, lemon juice zest, chilli and chicken.

🍲 Simmer for 25–30 minutes or until the chicken is tender. Serve with cooked long grain rice and green beans.

Spiced Chicken Drumettes (Ayam Goreng)

Makes about 12

Oil, for greasing and spraying
½ cup cornflour (corn starch)
2 teaspoons ground black pepper
½ teaspoon salt
1 teaspoon ground coriander/cilantro
1 teaspoon ground cumin
½ teaspoon ground chilli powder
1 kg/2 lb 3 oz lb chicken drumsticks
Sambal kecap or light soy sauce, to serve

🍲 Preheat the oven to 200°C/400°F.

🍲 Lightly grease a non-stick baking sheet with oil.

🍲 Combine the cornflour, pepper, salt, coriander/cilantror, cumin and chilli powder in a mixing bowl. Toss the chicken in the spice mixture to thoroughly coat.

🍲 Place the chicken on the prepared baking sheet, spray lightly with oil and bake for 20–25 minutes, or until golden and crisp. Serve with sambal kecap or light soy sauce.

Spicy Chicken Soup

Serves 4

4 cups low-salt chicken stock
4 kaffir lime leaves
2 stalks lemongrass
1 bunch fresh coriander/ cilantro with roots
8 thin slices fresh root ginger
2 skinless chicken breast fillets, cut into thin strips
4 French shallots, sliced
3 fresh birds-eye chillies or to taste
Pinch of sugar
4 tablespoons Thai fish sauce
Juice of 2 limes

🍲 Place the stock and 2 of the lime leaves in a large saucepan and bring to the boil.

🍲 Meanwhile, remove the outer layers of lemongrass and chop finely. Cut the roots from two of the coriander/cilantro plants. Remove the leaves from the remaining coriander/cilantro and set aside.

☕ Place the lemongrass, coriander/cilantro roots, remaining lime leaves and ginger in a mortar. Bruise with a pestle.

☕ Add the lemongrass mixture to the stock. Bring to simmering.

☕ Simmer for 2–3 minutes. Add the chicken and French shallots. Simmer for 5–6 minutes or until the chicken is cooked.

☕ Place the reserved coriander/cilantro leaves, chillies, sugar, fish sauce and lime juice in a small bowl. Mix to combine.

☕ To serve, divide the mixture between warm soup bowls. Remove the stalks of lemongrass from the soup and ladle over. Mix gently to combine. For a main meal, serve with steamed jasmine rice.

Thai Grilled Chicken

Serves 4–6

2 cloves garlic, crushed
1½ teaspoons ground coriander
2 teaspoons turmeric
Salt and freshly ground black pepper
2 tablespoons oil
500 g/1 lb 2 oz chicken wings
Coriander /cilantro chopped to garnish
Sweet chilli sauce

🍳 Mix the garlic, ground coriander/cilantro, turmeric, salt, pepper and oil together. Rub over the chicken. Set aside for at least 30 minutes, or cover and refrigerate overnight for a minimum of 4 hours if you can.

🍳 Heat a grill or BBQ. Grill the marinated chicken pieces until the juices run clear when tested.

🍳 Serve garnished with chopped coriander/cilantro and sweet chilli sauce.

Note: Can also be done in an air fryer or in the oven.

Chicken Yakitori

Makes 20 skewers

500 g/1 lb 2 oz skinless chicken breast fillets, thinly sliced
½ cup soy sauce
¼ cup honey
1 clove garlic, crushed
½ teaspoon ground ginger
Small bamboo skewers, soaked in water for 20 minutes

🍲 Place the sliced chicken in a glass bowl. Mix in the soy sauce, honey, garlic and ginger. Cover and place in the fridge to marinate for several hours or overnight.

🍲 Thread one or two strips onto each skewer, using a weaving motion. Brush with the reserved marinade.

🍲 Heat grill or BBQ to high. Grease rack or plate with oil and arrange the skewers in a row. Cook for 2½ minutes on each side, brushing with marinade as they cook.

🍲 Garnish with sesame seeds if desired and add your favorite dipping sauce.

🍲 Serve immediately.

Chicken Teriyaki

Serves 4

2 tablespoons butter
100 ml/3 fl oz teriyaki sauce or soy sauce
2.5 cm/1 in piece of ginger, chopped
2 tablespoons sugar
2 tablespoons dry sherry
500 g/1 lb 2 oz boneless chicken breasts, skinned
8 spring onions/scallions, cut into 2.5 cm/1 in strips
Bamboo skewers, soaked in water for 20 minutes

🍲 Place butter, teriyaki sauce, ginger, sugar and dry sherry in a small pan over a medium heat and stir until the sugar is dissolved. Leave to cool.

🍲 Cut the chicken into 2.5 cm/1 in pieces and stir into the marinade with the shallots. Chill for at least 2 hours.

🍲 Thread the chicken and spring onions/scallions onto the skewers and grill for 4–5 minutes on either side, or until cooked, brushing occasionally with marinade.

🍲 Serve with steamed rice and salad. Sprinkle with sesame seeds.

Seafood

Sambal Fried Prawns/ Shrimp (Udang Goreng)

Serves 4

1 tablespoon vegetable oil
24 green prawns/shrimp, heads and shells removed
Cooked rice of your choose.

Paste

3 garlic cloves, chopped
3 medium chillies, deseeded and chopped
3 teaspoons root ginger, chopped
1 stalk lemongrass, chopped
1 teaspoon ground coriander
Pinch of salt
2 teaspoons vegetable oil

☙ Crush or pound the paste ingredients in a mortar with a pestle or use a food processor.

☙ Heat the oil in a wok or frying pan. Add the prawns/shrimp and paste, and stir-fry for 3–4 minutes, or until cooked.

☙ Serve with rice.

Prawns/Shrimp in Hot Sauce (Sambal Udang)

Serves 4

500 g /1 lb 2 oz raw prawns/shrimp
20 cluster beans, approximately 5 pods (available from Indian stores)
2 cups coconut milk
4 potatoes, peeled and cut into wedges
1 tablespoon tamarind juice
1 teaspoon salt

Paste

5 spring onions/scallions
2 garlic cloves
5 red chillies, sliced
½ teaspoon shrimp paste (terasi)
2 tablespoons oil

🍲 Peel the prawns/shrimp and remove the intestinal tract. Open the bean pods and remove the beans.

🍲 Prepare the paste by grinding or pounding all the paste ingredients except for the oil. Heat the oil and sauté the spice paste until fragrant.

🍲 Add the prawns/shrimp and sauté until they change color, a few minutes. Add the beans and coconut milk and bring to the boil, stirring.

🍲 Add the potatoes and tamarind juice and simmer, uncovered, until the potatoes and shrimp are cooked and sauce has thickened.

🍲 Season with salt and serve.

Sambal Fried Snapper (Sambal Ikan Goreng)

Serves 4

1 teaspoon ground cumin
1 teaspoon ground coriander/cilantro
Zest of 1 lime, grated (shredded)
2 tablespoons lime juice
Salt, to taste
4 small snappers
⅓ cup plain flour
Peanut oil, for cooking

Marinade

2 spring onions/scallions, chopped
2 garlic cloves, chopped
2 teaspoons root ginger, chopped
2 medium chillies, deseeded and sliced

🍲 Grind or pound the marinade ingredients in a mortar with a pestle, or use a food processor. Add the cumin, coriander/cilantro, zest and lime juice and salt to the marinade.

🍲 Make two slits on each side of the snapper. Brush the mixture over the fish and marinate for 1 hour in the refrigerator.

🍲 Dip the fish in the flour.

🍲 Heat the oil in a wok or large frying pan. Fry the fish for 2–3 minutes on each side, or until crisp on the outside and cooked through.

🍲 Serve with the sambals (sauces) of your choice.

Chilli Crab with Lemongrass

Serves 2 - 4

1 large crab (1.3 kg/2.8 lbs) or 2 smaller crabs
1 tablespoon oil
2 cloves garlic, finely chopped
1 onion, sliced
1 stalk lemongrass, finely sliced
4 chillies, sliced
2 tablespoons fish sauce
2 tablespoons lime juice
½ cup water
4 spring onions/scallions, cut into 2.5 cm/1 in pieces
½ cup bean shoots and deep-fried shallots, to garnish
Extra lime juice and nuoc cham dipping sauce to serve

Clean the crab well.

🍲 Heat oil in a large saucepan, stir-fry garlic, onion, lemongrass and chilli over high heat for a few minutes.

🍲 Pour fish sauce, lime juice and water into the pan and bring to the boil.

☕ Carefully place crab in saucepan. Cover with a tightly fitting lid. Cook over a medium high heat for 10–15 minutes until the crab is cooked.

☕ Place crab on a serving platter. Add spring onions to the pan, heat cooking liquid until reduced to about ¼ cup and pour over the crab.

☕ Arrange bean shoots over the hot crab, sprinkle liberally with deep-fried shallots and serve with extra lime juice and dipping sauce.

Chinese Lobster Stir-Fry

Serves 4

500 g/1 lb 2 oz lobster meat, fresh or frozen
1 small clove garlic, minced
2 tablespoons oil
125 ml/4 fl oz chicken broth
1 small red capsicum/bell pepper
250 g/½ lb bean sprouts
250 g/½ lb water chestnuts
250 g/½ lb broccoli
370 g/12 oz Chinese cabbage, chopped
½ teaspoon salt
¼ teaspoon pepper
1 egg, beaten
Rice to serve

🍲 If frozen, thaw and chop lobster meat into bite-size pieces. In a pan sauté lobster and garlic in oil for 1 minute.

🍲 Add broth and vegetables and simmer, uncovered, for 5 minutes. Season with salt and pepper.

🍲 Add a little of the hot broth to lightly beaten egg. Stir the egg mixture into the rest of the broth. Heat gently but do not boil.

🍲 Serve with rice.

Fish in Banana Leaves (Ikan Panggang)

Serves 4

8 pieces banana leaf or kitchen foil
750 g /1 lb 9 oz boneless white fish fillets, diced
2 shallots, chopped
2 garlic cloves, chopped
1 tablespoon root ginger, chopped
¼ teaspoon ground turmeric
2 teaspoons ground coriander/cilantro

⅓ cup coconut milk
Juice of 1 lime
Salt, to taste
4 medium red chillies, deseeded and sliced
4 lime leaves, shredded
Lime wedges, to serve

🍲 Prepare the banana leaves by cutting into 15 cm/6 in square pieces. Dip each leaf in a bowl of boiling water.

🍲 Combine the fish, shallots, garlic, ginger, turmeric, coriander/cilantro, coconut milk, lime juice and salt in a food processor. Process until the mixture comes together.

🍲 Divide the mixture evenly into 8 and place in the middle of each banana leaf. Top with chilli and lime leaves. Fold banana leaf over fish, flatten a little and secure ends with cocktail sticks.

🍲 Cook the fish on a barbecue for 3 minutes on each side, or cook in a steamer for 3–4 minutes. Serve with wedges of lime.

Seafood Noodles

Serves 4

250 g/½ lb thin egg noodles
½ red capsicum/bell pepper, seeded
½ green capsicum/bell pepper, seeded
1 large squid tube, cleaned
2 teaspoons cornflour
2 tablespoons vegetable oil
Salt
Black pepper
1 teaspoon garlic, crushed
1 teaspoon ginger, crushed
1 spring onion/scallion, chopped
125 g/4 oz fresh mussels, cooked
8 oysters
1 ½ tablespoons soy sauce
1 ½ tablespoons dry sherry

🥥 In boiling salted water, cook noodles according to packet directions until al dente.

🥥 Rinse in cold water and drain. Cut capsicums/bell peppers into matchstick-thin lengths.

🥥 Cut squid into thin rings. Halve rings and toss in cornflour.

🥥 Heat oil in wok or frying-pan, add squid for 1 minute, stir-frying. Remove, drain on kitchen paper, lightly salt and liberally pepper it.

🥥 Add garlic, ginger, capsicums/bell peppers and spring onion/scallions to wok and stir-fry for 1 minute.

🥥 Add mussels, oysters, squid, soy sauce, dry sherry and noodles to stir-fry until heated through.

🥥 Pile onto warmed serving dish.

Singapore Chilli Crab

Serves 4

2 raw mud crabs, weighing about 1kg/2lb 3oz each
2 tablespoons sambal oelek (chilli paste)
⅓ cup tomato sauce
⅓ cup chilli sauce
2 tablespoons oyster sauce
1 tablespoon sugar
1 teaspoon salt
1 tablespoon vegetable oil
6 cloves garlic, minced
2 cups hot chicken stock
2 egg whites
¼ cup coriander/cilantro leaves

🦀 Cut the body section into 4 pieces and crack the large claw shells with the back of a heavy knife. Wash the crab and drain. Scrub the back shell and keep it whole to use as a garnish.

🦀 Combine the sambal oelek, tomato sauce and chilli sauce in a small bowl. Combine the oyster sauce, sugar and salt in another.

☕ Heat a wok over medium-high heat and add the oil. Fry the garlic for 10 seconds, stirring constantly. Add the chilli mixture and cook for another 10 seconds, stirring.

☕ Add the stock and oyster sauce mixture and stir again.

☕ Increase heat to high and bring to a fast boil. Add the crab pieces (including the back shell), stir to settle it into the liquid and cook for 3 minutes, stirring occasionally and turning the larger pieces once. Remove the back shell.

☕ Drizzle in the egg white and stir gently until there are white streaks through the sauce.

☕ Place on a serving dish, arrange the back shell on top and garnish with coriander/cilantro leaves.

☕ Serve with Chinese steamed or baked buns, rice or bread and a finger bowl.

Vegetables

Spinach with Peanut Sauce

Serves 4

750 g/25 oz water spinach or mature spinach
3 spring onions/scallions, sliced
2 cloves garlic, crushed
1 ½ tablespoons vegetable oil
¼ cup peanuts, crushed
Salt and pepper

Peanut sauce

⅓ cup smooth peanut butter
½ cup coconut milk
1 ½ tablespoons sugar
⅓ cup sweet chilli sauce
2 teaspoons lime or lemon juice
⅓ cup vegetable stock

To Garnish

Coriander/cilantro sprigs

🥥 Trim stalks of water spinach. Blanch spinach in boiling water to make it limp then place in cool or iced water. Drain completely

🥥 Make peanut sauce in saucepan by combining all ingredients and stirring over low heat until smooth.

🥥 Fry spring onions and garlic in oil until tender. Add peanuts and then spinach and peanut sauce.

🥥 Season with salt and pepper and garnish with coriander/cilantro sprigs.

Green Beans with Soy Sauce (Buncis Kecap)

Serves 4

1 tablespoon peanut oil
1 teaspoon sesame oil
1 garlic clove, crushed
2 shallots, sliced
300 g/11 oz green beans, trimmed and halved
2 tablespoons soy sauce
2 tablespoons water
1 cup beansprouts, trimmed
⅓ cup roasted peanuts, chopped

🥄 Heat the oil in a wok or frying pan. Add the sesame oil, garlic, shallots and beans.

🥄 Stir-fry for 2–3 minutes. Add the soy sauce and water and cook for 3–4 minutes, or until the beans are just cooked. Stir through the beansprouts and peanuts. Serve warm or cold.

Spicy Fried Eggplant (Terung Goreng)

Serves 4

½ cup peanut oil
2 eggplant/aubergines, cut into 1 cm /⅜ in slices
2 onions, sliced
2 garlic cloves, crushed
2 small chillies, deseeded and finely chopped
1 teaspoon ground coriander/cilantro
2 tablespoons tamarind concentrate
¼ cup water
1 teaspoon palm sugar or brown sugar
2 spring onions/scallions, sliced

Reserving 1 tablespoon of oil, brush the eggplant/aubergines slices with some of the remainder.

Heat a large non-stick frying pan. Add the eggplants/aubergines and cook for 1–2 minutes on each side until golden. Remove and set aside.

🍲 Heat the remaining oil. Add the onions and cook for 4–5 minutes, or until golden.

🍲 Add the garlic, chillies, coriander/cilantro, tamarind, water and sugar. Return the eggplant/aubergines to the pan and cook until the sauce reduces.

🍲 Garnish with spring onions/scallions.

🍲 Serve with side bowls of boiled rice.

Stir-Fried Vegetables

Serves 4

2 tablespoons vegetable or peanut oil
2 tablespoons of fresh root ginger, peeled and finely chopped
3 cloves garlic, peeled and finely chopped
2 tablespoons dry sherry
1 yellow capsicum/bell pepper, deseeded and chopped into 2.5 cm/1 in pieces
1 red capsicum/bell pepper, deseeded and chopped into 2.5 cm pieces/1 in pieces
2 medium carrots, peeled and thinly sliced on the diagonal
340 g/12 oz broccoli, cut into 2.5 cm/1 in florets and stalks thinly sliced
310 g/11 oz brown cap mushrooms, wiped and thickly sliced
2 tablespoons soy sauce
8 spring onions/scallions, cut into 1 cm/0.4 in diagonal slices
2 stalks celery cut into 1 cm pieces

🍵 Heat a large wok or heavy-based frying pan over a high heat for 1 minute. Add oil and rotate wok or pan to coat the base and lower sides.

🍵 Add ginger and garlic and stir-fry for 30 seconds. Add sherry and cook for a further 15 seconds. Add capsicums/bell peppers, celery and carrots and continue to stir-fry for 5 minutes or until vegetables start to soften.

🍵 Add broccoli, mushrooms and soy sauce, and stir-fry for 3 minutes or until all vegetables are just tender. Add spring onions/scallions and stir-fry for 1 minute.

🍵 Serve straight away.

Snow Peas with Garlic

Serves 6

315 g/11 oz snow peas
2 teaspoons garlic, crushed
2 teaspoons vegetable oil
¾ cup vegetable stock
1 teaspoon sugar
Salt
1 ¼ teaspoons cornflour
Garnish with sesame seeds

🍲 Bring water to the boil in a wok. Add snow peas and return to boil for 3 minutes. Strain.

🍲 Put oil in wok and quickly stir-fry garlic. Add snow peas, stock, sugar and salt to taste. Bring to the boil, stir, simmer for 2 minutes and remove snow peas to a serving dish.

🍲 Thicken stock with cornflour and pour over snow peas.

🍲 Sprinkle sesame seeds on top.

Rice & Noodles

Fried Rice (Nasi Goreng)

Serves 4

2 cups long-grain rice, rinsed
1 ½ tablespoons peanut oil
2 eggs, lightly beaten and a friend egg to top each serving
4 spring onions/scallions, finely sliced
2 garlic cloves, crushed
2 small red chillies, deseeded and finely chopped
300 g/11 oz chicken thigh fillets, diced
1 carrot, finely sliced or grated
1 small carrot, finely diced
100 g/3 ½ oz prawns/shrimps, peeled and cooked
2–3 tablespoons sweet soy sauce (kecap manis)
1 tablespoon soy sauce

🍚 Cook the rice in boiling salted water for 10–12 minutes, or until cooked. Drain and rinse.

🍚 Heat 2 teaspoons of the oil in a wok. Add the egg and swirl to coat the wok to form an omelette. Flip the omelette and cook the other side. Remove and cut into thin strips.

🍚 Heat the remaining oil in wok.

🍚 Add the spring onions/scallions, garlic and chilli and cook for 1–2 minutes. Add the chicken and stir-fry for 3 minutes.

🍚 Add the carrot, prawns/shrimp, kecap manis and soy sauce and stir-fry until the cabbage wilts.

🍚 Add the rice to the mixture and stir-fry until heated through. Serve rice with strips of omelette, fried shallots and the sambal (sauce) of your choice.

🍚 Or add a fried egg on top of each serving.

Yellow Rice (Nasi Kuning)

Serves 4

1 tablespoon vegetable oil
1 teaspoon ground turmeric
1 teaspoon ground coriander/cilantro
½ teaspoon ground cumin
2 cups long-grain rice, rinsed
2 cups coconut milk
1 cup water
6–8 curry leaves
1 cinnamon stick

 Heat the oil in a large saucepan. Add the turmeric, coriander/cilantro, cumin and rice. Stir for 1 minute to coat the rice and cook until aromatic.

 Add the coconut milk, water, curry leaves and cinnamon stick and bring to the boil.

 Reduce the heat to low and cook for 10–12 minutes or until the liquid is absorbed.

 Transfer the rice to a steamer and steam the rice for 12–15 minutes, stirring from time to time, or until the grains are light. If you don't have a steamer, continue to cook the rice on the lowest heat for 5–10 minutes, or until cooked. Remove the curry leaves and cinnamon stick and serve immediately.

Fragrant Rice (Nasi Gurih)

Serves 4

1 tablespoon vegetable oil
2 garlic cloves, crushed
6 spring onions/scallions, sliced
1 teaspoon ground coriander/cilantro
½ teaspoon galangal powder
2 cups long-grain rice, rinsed
2 cups coconut milk
½–1 cup water
6–8 curry leaves

☙ Heat the oil in a large saucepan. Add the garlic, spring onions/scallions, coriander/cilantro, galangal powder and rice. Stir for 1 minute to coat the rice and cook until aromatic.

☙ Add the coconut milk, water and curry leaves and bring to the boil. Reduce the heat to low and cook for 10 minutes, stirring from time to time, or until the liquid is absorbed. Transfer the rice to a steamer and steam for 10–12 minutes, or until the grains are light.

☙ If you don't have a steamer continue to cook the rice at the lowest heat for 5–10 minutes, or until cooked. Remove the curry leaves and serve immediately.

White Rice (Nasi Putih)

Serves 4

2 cups short-grain rice
2–3 cups water
1 teaspoon salt

🍚 Combine the rice, water and salt in a large saucepan. Bring to the boil.

🍚 Reduce the heat to very low, cover and allow to steam for 15 minutes, or until the rice is tender before serving.

Bacon Fried Rice

Serves 4

1 tablespoon olive oil
200 g/7 oz bacon, diced
3 cups cooked rice
add 2 spring onions/scallions, finely sliced

2 tablespoon soy sauce
1 clove garlic, crushed
2 tablespoons sweet chilli sauce

🍲 Heat the oil in a large wok. Lightly stir-fry bacon until lightly golden brown then add garlic and spring onions/scallions cook for 1 to 2 minutes and drain on a papertowel.

🍲 Add the rice and stir-fry until rice is hot. Add the bacon and mix well. Turn to very low heat and keep warm.

🍲 Add the rice, soy sauce and sweet chilli sauce and stir-fry until rice is hot, then turn to very low heat and keep warm. And add Spring onions/ Scallions just before serving to warm through.

Stir-fried Noodles with Pork & Ginger

Serves 2

500 g/1lb 2 oz Chinese egg noodles
250 g/½ lb minced pork
1 tablespoon soy sauce
1 tablespoon dry sherry
1 teaspoon corn-starch (cornflour)
2 tablespoons vegetable oil
2 spring onions/scallions, finely chopped, plus extra to garnish
1 teaspoon fresh root ginger, finely grated
1 carrot, finely chopped
3 tablespoons black bean sauce
150ml/5 fl oz chicken stock

🍲 Cook the noodles according to the packet instructions and then drain well.

🍲 In a bowl, mix together the pork, soy sauce, sherry and corn-starch. Stir well to combine.

🍵 Heat the oil in a wok or large heavy based frying pan, then add the scallions and ginger and stir-fry for 30 seconds. Add the pork mixture and carrot and stir-fry for 5–10 minutes, until the pork has browned. Stir in black bean sauce.

🍵 Pour in stock and bring to the boil. Add the noodles and cook, uncovered, for 3–5 minutes, until most of the liquid is absorbed and the noodles are piping hot.

🍵 Garnish with scallions.

Fried Noodles with Chicken

Serves 4

200 g/7 oz dried egg noodles or thin noodles
1 tablespoon peanut oil
4 shallots, sliced
500 g/1 lb 2 oz chicken thigh fillets, diced
2 garlic cloves, crushed
1 carrot, peeled and finely sliced or grated (shredded)
2 cups Chinese cabbage, shredded
2 tablespoons sweet soy sauce (kecap manis)
⅓ cup chicken stock
1 cup beansprouts
4 spring onions/scallions, sliced

🍲 Cook the noodles following the packet directions. Drain and set aside.

🍲 Heat the oil in a wok. Add the shallots and cook until golden. Add the chicken and garlic and stir-fry until just cooked.

🍲 Add carrots and stir-fry for another 2 minutes. Add the cabbage, kecap manis and stock and continue to cook until the cabbage is wilted.

🍲 Add the noodles, beansprouts and spring onions/scallions and stir-fry until heated through.

Bakmi Goreng Seafood

Serves 4

Heads and shells of 16 raw king prawns /shrimp, washed
1 teaspoon salt
16 raw king prawns/shrimp, shelled, tails intact
6 cups chicken stock
2 tablespoons peanut oil
6 French shallots, sliced
2 teaspoons sambal oelek (chilli paste)
200 g/7oz fresh egg noodles
2 handfuls bean sprouts
2 handfuls kangkung or Asian greens, sliced into
5 cm/2 in pieces
2 boiled eggs, sliced
2 fish cakes, sliced
16 slices cooked pork (optional)

Place the prawn/shrimp heads and shells in a pot with 2 cups water and the salt and bring to the boil. When just boiling, add the prawns/shrimps, reduce heat and simmer for 4 minutes.

Remove the prawns/shrimps and set aside. Meanwhile, bring the chicken stock to the boil and reduce to a simmer.

🍲 Strain the prawns/shrimps stock into the chicken stock and continue to simmer.

🍲 Heat a wok over medium heat and add the oil. Add the shallots and fry until browned and crisp. Add the sambal oelek and fry for about 3 minutes or until aromatic, stirring constantly. Add the contents of the wok to the stock with an extra teaspoon salt.

🍲 Bring a large pot of water to the boil. Cook noodles, bean sprouts and kangkung for about 30 seconds.

🍲 Drain and divide between 4 large soup bowls.

🍲 Top each with quarter of the boiled egg, fish cake, pork and cooked prawns/shrimps. Fill the bowls with chicken stock mixture.

🍲 Garnish with crispy fried shallots.

Fried Rice

Serves 4

500 g/1 lb 2 oz cooked and cooled white rice
2 eggs
Vegetable oil
250 g/½ lb streaky bacon, diced
250 g prawns/shrimps/½ lb, cooked and chopped
5 mushrooms, thinly sliced
4 spring onions/scallions, chopped
Salt and pepper, to taste
4 teaspoons soy sauce

🥥 Beat eggs lightly in a bowl, then heat 1 teaspoon of oil in a frying pan and fry the eggs as a thin pancake or omelette. Remove from pan and slice into strips. (If you prefer, eggs can be beaten and added to the rice later.)

🥥 Cook the bacon and set aside.

🍲 Place enough oil in a large pan to cover the base and heat it. When hot, add the rice and stir fry for about 4–5 minutes or until rice is thoroughly heated through. Stir regularly, breaking up any lumps.

🍲 Add prawns/shrimp, mushrooms, spring onions/scallions (reserving some to garnish), and salt and pepper, then fold in egg pieces (or beaten egg) and soy sauce. Mix well.

🍲 Top with bacon and remaining shallots and serve.

Index

First published in 2023 by New Holland Publishers, Sydney
Level 1, 178 Fox Valley Road, Wahroonga, 2076, NSW, Australia

newhollandpublishers.com

A record of this book is held at the National Library of Australia

ISBN 9781760792855

Managing Director: Fiona Schultz
Production Director: Arlene Gippert

Printed in China

10 9 8 7 6 5 4 3 2 1

Keep up with New Holland Publishers

        NewHollandPublishers

 @newhollandpublishers